D1200568

Let's Hear It For

GREAT DANES

Robin Koontz

Educational Media

rourkeeducationalmedia.com

*Scan for Related Titles
and Teacher Resources*

Before Reading:

Building Academic Vocabulary and Background Knowledge

Before reading a book, it is important to tap into what your child or students already know about the topic. This will help them develop their vocabulary, increase their reading comprehension, and make connections across the curriculum.

1. *Look at the cover of the book. What will this book be about?*
2. *What do you already know about the topic?*
3. *Let's study the Table of Contents. What will you learn about in the book's chapters?*
4. *What would you like to learn about this topic? Do you think you might learn about it from this book? Why or why not?*
5. *Use a reading journal to write about your knowledge of this topic. Record what you already know about the topic and what you hope to learn about the topic.*
6. *Read the book.*
7. *In your reading journal, record what you learned about the topic and your response to the book.*
8. *After reading the book complete the activities below.*

Content Area Vocabulary
Read the list. What do these words mean?

ancestors
Assyrians
breed
brindle
descendants
ferocious
mobility

After Reading:

Comprehension and Extension Activity

After reading the book, work on the following questions with your child or students in order to check their level of reading comprehension and content mastery.

1. What are some surprising personality traits of a Great Dane? Why are they surprising? (Summarize)
2. Why do some people crop the ears of Great Danes? (Infer)
3. Why don't Great Danes live to be very old? (Asking questions)
4. Would a Great Dane be the right dog for you? Why or why not? (Text to self)
5. What do you think are the most important things to teach a dog? (Asking questions)

Extension Activity

Read more about the three ancestors of the Great Dane. What traits do they have in common with the modern Great Dane? Draw a diagram that shows the common traits.

Table of Contents

Great Danes

Even people who don't know much about dogs usually know a Great Dane when they see one! Great Danes are sometimes called "the Apollo of all Dogs." Apollo was a powerful Greek god.

Great Dane Facts

Weight: 100-200 pounds (45-90 kilograms)

Height: 28-34 inches (71-86 centimeters)

Country of Origin: Germany

Life Span: 7-9 years

The large and noble Great Dane is more commonly called a gentle giant. That is a perfect description for this sweet-natured dog that can grow as big as a small horse!

People tend to step aside when a Great Dane passes by. It's no wonder these dogs were often used as guard dogs.

Surprisingly, Great Danes are not the tallest dog **breed**. That honor goes to the Irish Wolfhound, with Danes running a close second. Still, the tallest dog ever recorded was a Great Dane named Zeus. Zeus measured 44 inches (112 centimeters) from paw to shoulder. He was as big as a donkey! Three previous world record-holders were also Great Danes.

Irish Wolfhound

Look at Me!

A Great Dane has a massive head and a long, graceful neck. It has a sleek, muscular body, deep chest, and long legs and tail. Great Danes are built so well they can walk, trot, and run with balance and elegance despite their massive size.

Great Danes appear in several colors. They can be fawn (tan), blue (gray), **brindle**, black, or the popular harlequin mix, which is mostly white with black patches.

Upright ears can give Great Danes an even more fearsome appearance. But these dogs are born with long, floppy ears. People once cropped the ears of Great Danes to prevent injury while they hunted wild boars. Ear cropping has been banned in many countries since the dogs are no longer used to hunt dangerous animals.

When ears are cropped, about two-thirds of the earflap is sliced off by a veterinarian. The remaining ear is taped up until it stands on its own.

History of the Great Dane

Dogs similar to Great Danes have been with us for a long time. There are drawings of them on Egyptian monuments over 5,000 years old. The dogs are described in Chinese literature from 1121 BCE. Similar dogs are pictured on Greek money dating back to 36 BCE.

Assyrians from the Middle East invaded parts of what are now Germany, Italy, and Spain. The attackers brought powerful dogs with them.

English Mastiff

Irish Wolfhounds

The huge dogs were so fierce they could hunt down and kill a **ferocious** wild boar.

These tough hunting dogs are believed to have been a mixture of an Irish Wolfhound and English Mastiff. Years later, people matched the powerful breed with the sleek, fast Greyhound. Their puppies were the first of the modern Great Danes.

Wild boars are savage animals with razor-sharp teeth and tusks. Anything that attacks a wild boar has to be strong and brave.

Greyhound

Often called Boar Hounds, Great Danes were used for hunting and for guarding homes. German nobles called the beautiful dogs *Kammerhunde*, which means "chamber dog." The guard dogs wore fancy collars and lived pampered lives on huge estates.

The favored chamber dog was trusted to protect its sleeping masters from possible harm.

Throughout the 1800s, German breeders refined the Great Dane breed. They paired dogs that were not as aggressive. They were able to produce puppies that were more loving and gentle. Those less aggressive **descendants** of the original Boar Hounds were the **ancestors** of the Great Danes we know and adore today.

People from Denmark brought German Boar Hounds into their country. A famous French traveler saw the dogs and called them *Grand Danois*, or "Great Dane."

Working Danes

The American Kennel Club (AKC) categorizes Great Danes in the working dog group. This is because of their long history of hunting and guarding. Most Great Danes are now kept as companion pets, but some are also working dogs.

Great Danes are often trained to become therapy dogs. Therapy dogs must be smart, patient, and gentle with people. A Great Dane can be a natural therapy dog!

Great Danes are popular in "Read to a Dog" and similar reading programs in schools.

Danes and their owners work together to help all sorts of people. The gentle giants visit hospitals and nursing homes. They bring joy and companionship to the patients and their families.

Strong and well-mannered, Great Danes can be trained to become excellent helpers for those with **mobility** issues. People with balance problems, limb loss, and other challenges have Great Danes to help them.

The big and friendly Great Dane's easy-going, loving personality also helps people who feel isolated and depressed.

A Loyal Companion

Great Danes are friendly, affectionate, and kind dogs. Danes are playful and gentle, making them terrific with children and other pets. They also accept strangers as long as they don't see a threat to their family.

Large dogs like Great Danes tend to have a shorter life span than small dogs. Great Danes are also prone to a life-threatening health condition called bloat, or gastric torsion.

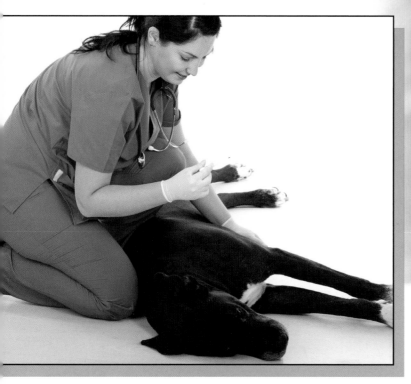

Regular visits to the vet help keep a pet happy and healthy.

Like all dogs, Great Danes need consistent training to learn good manners. A dog is a pack animal that needs a leader. If the human isn't behaving like a good leader, then the dog might try to establish its own rules of behavior.

It's important to train a Great Dane while it is still a puppy and smaller than its human. The good news is that Great Danes are fairly easy to train and eager to please. But be careful, some Danes believe they should be lap dogs!

Great Danes are mellow and quiet enough to be an excellent housedog. The house just needs to be big enough for them.

Doggie Advice

Puppies are cute and cuddly, but adopting one should never be done without serious thought. Choosing the right breed of dog requires some homework. And remember that a dog will require more than love and great patience. It will require food, exercise, grooming, a safe place to live, and medical care.

A dog can be your best friend, but you need to be its best friend, too. For more information about adopting and owning a dog, contact the American Kennel Club at www.akc.org or the Canadian Kennel Club at www.ckc.ca.

Glossary

ancestors (AN-seh-sturs): members of a family who lived long ago

Assyrians (uh-SIHR-ee-uhns): ancient people from the 14th-6th century BCE who lived in what is now northern Iraq and southeastern Turkey

breed (BREED): particular kind of domestic animal within a larger, closely related group

brindle (BRIN-dul): hard-to-see streaks of dark color on a lighter background

descendants (di-SEND-uhnts): people, plants, or animals that are descended from a particular ancestor

ferocious (fuh-ROH-shuhss): very fierce and savage

mobility (moh-BIL-uh-tee): the ability to move

Index

Show What You Know

1. Why are people sometimes afraid of a Great Dane?
2. What jobs did Great Danes do for humans in the past?
3. What jobs does a Great Dane do today?

Websites to Visit

national.gdac.org

www.dogbreedinfo.com/greatdane.htm

www.akc.org/dog-breeds/great-dane/detail

About the Author

Robin Koontz is an author/ illustrator of a variety of books for kids. She lives with her husband in the Coast Range of western Oregon where their Border Collie, Jeep, keeps a close eye on her. You can learn more on Robin's blog: robinkoontz.wordpress.com.

Meet The Author!
www.meetREMauthors.com

www.rourkeeducationalmedia.com

PHOTO CREDITS: Cover: Photohunter; Pages 4-5 © Dmussman, inset photo © Eric Isselee; page 6 © Daniele Vannini, page 7 © Manfred Ruckszio; page 8 © volofin, page 9 dog with puppies © Erik Lam, bottom photo © Vtls; page 10 © DragoNika, page 10-11 © Waldemar Dabrowski, page 11 © Xseon; map page 13 © pavalena, photo page 13 © Grigvovan; page 14 child reading © Flashon Studio, © dog Nathalie Photography, page 15 © Eric Isselee; page 16 © Susan Schmitz, page 16-17 © Geoff Goldswain; page 18 © Blaj Gabriel; page 20 © Yura Dobro, page 21 © Maja H.

All photos from Shutterstock.com except page 11 top © Tkoletsis https://creativecommons.org/licenses/by-sa/3.0/deed.en , page 18-19 © Szabolcs Stieber | Dreamstime.com

Edited by: Keli Sipperley

Cover design and layout: Nicola Stratford   www.nicolastratford.com

Library of Congress PCN Data

Let's Hear It For Great Danes / Robin Koontz
(Dog Applause)
ISBN 978-1-68342-170-2 (hard cover)
ISBN 978-1-68342-238-9 (e-Book)
Library of Congress Control Number: 2016956598

Printed in the United States of America, North Mankato, Minnesota

Also Available as:
ROURKE'S
e-Books